# AND IT WAS SO

## Words from the Scripture

*ILLUSTRATED BY TASHA TUDOR*

THE WESTMINSTER PRESS
PHILADELPHIA

First published by The Westminster Press 1958

The references are: p.3, Gen. 1:1; p.4, Gen. 1:3; pp.5-6, Gen. 1:5; p.7, Gen. 1:16; p.8, Gen. 1:9; p.9, Gen. 1:11; p.10, Gen. 1:21b; p.11, Gen. 1:25; p.12, Gen. 1:27-29; p.13, Gen. 1:30; p.14, Gen. 1:31; p.15, Gen. 2:1a; p.16, Ps. 147:7a; p.17, Ps. 147:1b; pp.18-21, Ps. 147:8-9; p.22, Ps. 147:16a; p.23, Ps. 147:18b; p.24, Eccl. 3:11a,17b,2; p.25, Eccl. 3:3b-7; p.26, Ps. 24:1; p.27, Ps. 66:1-2a; p.28, Isa. 9:6, Luke 1:31; pp.30-31, 1 John 4:19; pp.32-33, I John 4:7a; p.34, Acts 10:38b; p.35, Mark 1:32, 34; p.36, Mark 4:1; p.37, Mark 4:2; pp.38-39, Matt. 19:13-14a; p.40, Matt. 21:10-11; p.41, Matt. 21:15; p.42, Matt. 28:19; p.43, Matt. 28:20; pp.44-45, Ps. 122:1; pp.46-47, Ps. 46:10; p.48, Ps. 18:1a, 49b.

Second edition
Published by The Westminster Press
Philadelphia, Pennsylvania

**Library of Congress Cataloging-in-Publication Data**

And it was so.

SUMMARY: An illustrated collection of Bible verses, some of which have been adapted.
1. Creation—Biblical teaching—Juvenile literature.
2. Jesus Christ—Juvenile literature. [1. Bible—Selections] I. Tudor, Tasha, ill.
BS651.A56 1988    220.5′20426    87-16130
ISBN 0-664-32724-9

Printed in Singapore

In the beginning God created the heavens and the earth.

And God said, "Let there be light"; and there was light.

And God called the light Day,

and the darkness God called Night.

And God made two great lights, to rule the day
and to rule the night; God made the stars also.

And God said, "Let the waters be gathered together and let the dry land appear."

And God said, "Let the earth put forth plants yielding seed
and trees bearing fruit."

And God created every winged bird according to its kind.

And God made the beasts of the earth, and cattle,
and everything that creeps upon the ground.

God created man and woman and blessed them, and said to them, "Behold, I have given you every plant yielding seed which is upon the face of all the earth, and every tree with seed in its fruit; you shall have them for food."

"And to every beast of the earth, and to every bird of the air, and to everything that creeps on the earth, everything that has the breath of life, I have given every green plant for food."

And God saw everything that was made,
and it was very good.

Thus the heavens and the earth were finished.

Sing to the Lord with thanksgiving.

For it is good to sing praises to our God.

God covers the heavens with clouds.

God prepares rain for the earth.

God makes grass grow upon the hills.

God gives to the beasts their food,
and to the young ravens which cry.

God gives snow like wool.

God makes the wind blow, and the waters flow.

God has made everything beautiful
   in its time.
For God has appointed a time
   for every matter,
   and for every work:
a time to plant, and a time to
   pluck up what is planted;

a time to break down, and a time to build up;
a time to weep, and a time to laugh;
a time to mourn, and a time to dance;
a time to seek, and a time to lose;
a time to keep, and a time to cast away;
a time to keep silence, and a time to speak.

The earth is the Lord's and the fulness thereof,
the world and those who dwell therein.

Make a joyful noise to God, all the earth;
sing the glory of God's name.

For to us a child is born,
to us a son is given.

And you shall call his name Jesus.

We love,

because God first loved us.

Let us love one another,

for love is of God.

Jesus went about doing good, for God was with him.

They brought to him all who were sick,
and he healed many.

Jesus began to teach beside the sea. And a very large crowd gathered about him, so that he got into a boat and sat in it.

And Jesus taught them many things.

Then children were brought to him that he might lay his
hands on them and pray.

The disciples rebuked the people; but Jesus said,
"Let the children come to me."

And when Jesus entered Jerusalem, the crowds said,
"This is Jesus."

And the children in the temple cried out, "Hosanna!"

And Jesus said, "Go, teach all nations."

And Jesus said, "I am with you always."

I was glad when they said to me,

"Let us go to the house of the Lord!"

Be still, and know that I am God.

I am exalted in the earth.

I love you, O Lord,
and sing praises to your name.